CW01430263

Absolute Crime Presents:

The Death Row Cookbook

The Famous Last Meals (With Recipes) of Death Row Convicts

ABSO UTE CR ME

By John Fleury

Absolute Crime Books

www.absolutecrime.com

Cover Image © darren whittingham - Fotolia

Table of Contents

About Us

Absolute Crime publishes only the best true crime literature. Our focus is on the crimes that you've probably never heard of, but you are fascinated to read more about. With each engaging and gripping story, we try to let readers relive moments in history that some people have tried to forget.

Remember, our books are not meant for the faint at heart. We don't hold back — if a crime is bloody, we let the words splatter across the page so you can experience the crime in the most horrifying way!

If you enjoy this book, please visit our homepage to see other books we offer; if you have any feedback, we'd love to hear from you!

Introduction

The last meals of death row convicts fascinate us because they offer an insight into a disturbed mind shortly before its owner's death. The last meal is a way for the system to offer a last minute nod to humanity; that although these murderers, rapists, and villains listed below may have performed inhuman acts, they are still indeed human. The irony of feeding a criminal before killing them by electrocution or lethal injection is not missed on many of the inmates, as we shall see from some of their choices. Controversial and fascinating, the last meals of the condemned will continue to make headlines as long as the death penalty exists.

The Chefs behind the Final Meal

Death Row and Capital Punishment

"Death Row" refers to the cordoned-off section of a prison - most likely a maximum-security prison - where the people being detained there have been accused and found guilty of a crime that warrants capital punishment. Not all countries in the world have laws condoning, accepting, or enforcing capital punishment, but if it is an option for sentencing, and the deciding party believes that death is the only rightful consequence for the person being accused, it is possible. The members of that deciding party must consent by a majority to enforce this punishment upon the accused.

Many people refer to and understand the phrase "capital punishment" to mean a death sentence - and they are completely correct. In many different countries, capital punishment is an incredibly sensitive and controversial topic that, if brought up in conversation, can lead to very public and very heated arguments.

Many people have staunch personal opinions on the subject. Not so many people give much thought to those whose job it is to actually cook and deliver a last meal to a death row inmate.

Inside Death Row Kitchens

How can a chef stand to make a meal for a person who was convicted of a crime so abhorrent that it has been deemed right for that person to die?

Just because death row inmates don't have as many rights as the average person who is still allowed to walk free and live his or her life, the general thought is that those who are incarcerated and awaiting certain death still have the right to privacy, even if it is limited. It may not be widely publicized, but all ethics aside, it is fairly certain that the chef who is responsible for cooking that inmate's last meal knows exactly the crimes that were committed.

What happens if the chef personally knows someone who has suffered that same crime? What if the chef has actually been a victim of that particular crime? The chef may happen to be a victim of a similar crime that was committed. The chef may have personal knowledge of a victim of a similar type of crime. The chef may even have a close relative - a wife, son, or daughter - who was a victim of the same type of crime. How does the chef cope with the fact that he or she is duty-bound to cook a nourishing meal for a person who willingly hurt another human being - or many other human beings - and will just die soon enough anyway?

Is it immoral for the chef to spit in the inmate's last meal? Is it immoral for the chef to do something worse to the food, such as undercook it, or do something that makes it taste bad? Would anyone who is in the kitchen with the chef even care which horrible or untoward things are done to that inmate's last meal?

When we look at these questions in an objective sense, the majority of people would most likely feel some sort of remorse or guilt if they did anything like that to another human being's very last meal. However, the chef is around those death row inmates for the majority of the day. The inmates are not going to be kind or civil to anyone who keeps them locked up and in constant confinement day in and day out, whether they are guilty or not.

Inmates may start their death row sentence with the best of intentions, in order to atone for the crime or crimes committed, but no human being can stay completely positive in such a horrible environment for such a long time. In the United States penal system, the average length of time that an inmate must wait on death row to be eventually executed has increased substantially ever since execution became an accepted practice. As of 2010, the average waiting time for a death row inmate, between sentencing and the actual execution, was 178 months. (Source: Bureau of Justice Statistics, http://bjs.ojp.usdoj.gov/index.cfm?ty=pbdetail&iid=2236)

Unless the chef is a saint, he or she will feel a sense of loathing from those inmates on a daily basis. Yet, he or she still needs to serve the condemned as part of his or her job description.

Back in the "Real" World

After dealing with the daily, arduous duty of the job description, the chef is finally allowed to go home and rest. But can it really be called rest?

Working as a chef who cooks the final meals for death row inmates sparks millions of questions from the people who are supposed to be his or her friends. The constant barrage of questions and comments being thrown in the chef's face can be unbearable:

"What is it like? Have you met anyone interesting?"

"Oh, my GOD, I could NEVER do that sort of thing! I would absolutely HATE my job!"

"What happens if you just KNOW that one of those...people...is innocent?"

Even the questions and comments which might have been meant to show sympathy or add a bit of light can make the chef feel out of sorts. Prison guards and chefs can become despondent from the stress of dealing with death row itself and its hateful inmates, the confinement of the kitchen, and the job itself. It may feel like a never-ending and ever-growing weight that will just not let up.

Psychological Training

In addition to the usual training for a person to work within the prison system - extensive physical and safety training - a death row chef must undergo psychological training. The damage to the mental health of the chef is clear if psychological training is not taken seriously.

As with former members of any military force who have been to war and seen it firsthand, PTSD (Post-Traumatic Stress Disorder) is a possibility for these valiant chefs if every aspect of their health is not checked, assessed, and treated properly on a regular basis. Though these chefs are not on foreign lands, they still endure frontline battle every day that they are on the job. They are surrounded by prison guards - who were most likely in the military at some point in their lives - carrying heavy-duty guns and other weaponry. They must be escorted through each and every hallway in order to serve the last meals to the inmates. They must be locked inside all day with people - inmates OR guards - who may or may not become violent at any point.

These chefs haven't committed any crime, but they may rightfully feel like prisoners themselves.

A Firsthand Account

The Guardian published a piece about a man named Brian Price in 2004. Price was exposed to all of these aforementioned hardships and many more because, "For 11 years, Brian Price was the man responsible for preparing the last meal requests in Texas." Price wrote a book where he covered about his feelings while performing his duties and the emotions he experienced during different interactions. His account confirmed the difficulty of performing this role.

We will never experience the thoughts that go through such a chef's mind, or understand how those workplace experiences affect that person's life.

The death penalty has always been a controversial policy that has its backers and haters, and the last meal of the condemned manages to strike a chord with many people as it is a suggestion that those being put to death, no matter their crime, are still human. We put people to death for the terrible crimes they've committed, and at the same time feed them the meals they love. It is this irony that will continue to fascinate us all as long as the death penalty is in place.

Hastings Arthur Wise

Hastings Arthur Wise was born on February 16, 1954 and was a convicted U.S. mass murderer who was executed in South Carolina for killing four former coworkers. Wise shot and killed Charles Griffeth, David Moore, Leonard Filya, and Sheryl Wood on September 15, 1997 at the R.E. Phelon Company, which is a manufacturing factory in Aiken, South Carolina.

Wise was a former employee at the company and produced lawnmower parts for the company prior to the workplace shooting. He was an ex-convict who had served prison time for bank robbery and fencing (receiving and selling stolen goods). After his release, he obtained a technical degree and found a job at R.E. Phelon because had no criminal convictions for over a decade before joining the company.

The motives for his crimes and murders are simple, and stem from his termination of employment from the factory following a confrontation with a supervisor weeks earlier. Before the shooting, Wise eerily warned his boss and co-workers that he would "be back." On September 15, 1997, he returned to the R.E. Phelon factory and opened fire, killing four and injuring three.

Wise was indicted in August 1998 and his trial was delayed because of changes in counsel and the presiding judge. Furthermore, the trial was moved to an adjacent county because of pre-trial publicity. Race also played a role in the trial, since Wise was black.

After conviction, media and external parties asserted that racism played a role in the sentence and verdict. However, Wise, rather unusually, made a request to the state Supreme Court to waive all his further appeals of his death sentence. In fact, he claimed that his second appeal was made against his wishes and that he wished to die. He refused to participate and pursue all his permitted appeals, and Wise became a "volunteer" for execution, who some claim is a sign of mental defect and depression. Ex parte motions to challenge his competency to be executed were filed, since execution of the mentally diminished is (now) illegal in the United States. However, all the motions were rejected and the sentenced stayed.

Wise was convicted and sentenced to death in South Carolina by lethal injection. While at the Broad River Correctional Institution, Wise was granted a final meal request by the prison officials. On the day of his execution, which was Friday, November 4, 2005, Wise requested a final meal of lobster back, coleslaw, and French fries, followed by banana pudding and milk. On November 4, 2005, he was executed by lethal injection and made no final statement before his execution.

Hastings Arthur Wise's Lobster Back

Any part of a lobster is a delicacy. But the lobster back is where you find the lobster meat that offers the best taste. Also, preparing lobster back is simple, and it should take you a maximum of 10 minutes. This means you can thrill your family members and friends easily by serving them perfect homemade lobster back.

Ingredients:

- 4-6 frozen lobster tails (1-2 per person)
- Butter
- Lemon slices

Preparation:

It's important to defrost the lobster back fully before cooking, even if you feel more comfortable handling frozen lobsters.

1. Preheat the oven to 350 F.
2. Cut the defrosted lobster back, and place them on a baking sheet.
3. Brush each piece with butter.
4. Bake for about 15 minutes, but make sure you don't overcook it as that can leave the end product hard and rubbery.

5. After removing the lobster back from the oven, add melted butter and lemon slices to make it soft and sweet.

While it's advisable to serve cooked lobster back without delay, you can always keep them in your refrigerator for up to two days.

Ted Bundy

Theodore Robert "Ted" Bundy was a serial killer, kidnapper, rapist, and necrophile, who murdered young women during the 1970's. Although he denied his involvement in multiple murders, he ultimately confessed to killing over 30 people in the 1970's, and although he was proven to have committed these murders, countless other still-open homicides are believed to have been committed by Bundy.

Ted Bundy was born on November 24, 1946, and despite the gruesome nature of his crimes did not have a life of crime. Bundy had a "normal" childhood and attended college in Washington. Described as hard working and empathetic by some, Bundy worked on political campaigns, but it was while in law school he began to exhibit strange behavior. It was also during this time in 1974 that young women began to disappear in the Pacific Northwest.

Many of his victims were young women, and some victims were kept nearby, where Bundy would visit them and perform sexual acts on the corpses until the body became putrefied or destroyed by wildlife.

The gruesome nature of the crimes and his treatment of the victims made Bundy one of the most notorious serial killers during his time and in American history, and his pathology and criminal behavior are studied by psychologists and law enforcement to this day.

Bundy was convicted of only a few murders, but would subsequently confess to over 30 and be suspected of committing close to 100 murders in his lifetime. He would appear to be a normal, charming, and even charismatic man in public, but beneath his façade there was a more sinister side. Experts who interviewed Bundy while he was incarcerated were unable to precisely diagnose the man, but the evidence pointed away from schizophrenia and other psychoses and in fact, many believe he had antisocial personality disorder.

Patients with antisocial personality disorder are frequently identified as "sociopaths" or "psychopaths" and many believe they have no conscious or value for human life. As such, they are considered incurable and a danger to society.

Like most states, Florida offers its condemned inmates a last meal request and a final statement prior to the execution. Bundy, though, declined a special last meal, and simply requested a meal chosen by the death row officers. The officers overseeing Florida's death row opted to give Bundy a "traditional" last meal. This last meal consisted of steak cooked medium rare, eggs cooked over easy, toast with butter and jelly, hash browns, milk, and juice. Ted Bundy did not give a final statement prior to his execution.

Ted Bundy's Medium Rare Steak

Ingredients:

- 1 large steak
- 2 tablespoons of olive oil
- 2 cloves of garlic
- 1/4 cup of teriyaki sauce
- Salt
- Pepper

Preparation:

1. Take the steak and place it in a large Ziploc bag with a 1/4 cup of teriyaki sauce and 2 cloves of coarsely chopped garlic.
2. Allow it to sit for at least 2 hours in the refrigerator.
3. Remove it from the refrigerator, and allow it to sit at room temperature for 30 minutes.
4. Remove the steak from the bag and add salt and pepper to taste.
5. Rub the steak with olive oil.
6. Heat a frying pan to a medium-high temperature and place the steak in the pan.
7. Cook the steak for about 4 minutes and flip it. Cook the steak for another 4 minutes. For an exact medium-rare steak, aim for an internal temperature of 145 degrees F.
8. Serve it with a delicious accompanying dish of your choice.

John Wayne Gacy

John Wayne Gacy was executed by the state of Illinois on May 10, 1994. Allegedly, his last words, spoken in spite to the executioner (by lethal injection), were 'Kiss my ass'. Gacy, as with all other death row inmates (up until quite recently), was allowed two things at the approach of his execution date: a religious figure, and a last meal request. Many people request meals they would have enjoyed prior to their incarceration. Some people make statements with their meal choice (a single olive pit, a pizza donated to a homeless shelter, etc.). Gacy, in true 'Gacy' fashion, ordered the following: 12 fried shrimp, bucket of original KFC fried chicken (Gacy had managed several Kentucky Fried Chicken restaurants prior to his discovery as a sadistic serial rapist/murderer, his wife's father had owned a string of chains throughout the Midwestern United States), French fries, and one full pound of strawberries.

There was no order to this meal. Similar to his murders, his attention was thrown out the window, and Gacy attacked the meal all at once, everything thrown into one silver-aluminum disposable container.

Gacy's meal was not all that strange in comparison to others' choices. Perhaps a little on the heavy side at 250+ pounds, his meal was larger than most, yet the food rather tame in comparison to his crimes. Dressed as a clown named Pogo, Gacy would entertain church gatherings, Boy Scout events, and children's parties in the decades prior to his arrest. Occasionally, he would hire young men to work on construction crews that he would generate, for his house or those of friends and relatives who trusted him.

Many of these young men were later discovered deceased, rotting in the crawlspace beneath his house. Several of his victims were discovered to have been thrown into the Des Plaines River. Numerous victims have yet to be identified, as Gacy's under-the-radar operations and frequent travel, combined with his execution and suspected use of an accomplice, have metaphorically thrown a wrench into the works.

Pogo, the clown devised by Gacy himself, remains synonymous to this day of John's crimes. A majority of Gacy's victims were discovered to have died by strangulation or asphyxiation, brought on by Gacy's descriptions of the tricks he would perform as Pogo. Many consider his 'handcuff-escape' trick a key to the methodology of his after-hour crimes, incapacitating his unaware young men within his house, raping, then strangling them to death. A strong indication of Gacy's guilt was his prior criminal activity. While the murders he is suspected of committing occurred from 1974-1978, Gacy was accused and highly suspected of committing sexual abuse towards young men several times in the late 1960s, leading many experts in this field to consider Gacy a prime suspect in the later disappearance of many other young men in the Chicago (and surrounding) areas.

John Wayne Gacy's KFC-Style Fried Chicken

Whenever we talk of fried chicken, it's Kentucky that comes to your mind in the first instance. Such is the universal acclamation KFC has gained over the years, ensuring that people who want the authentic taste don't turn elsewhere. How about trying KFC-style fried chicken at home? It's not as difficult as you may presume.

Ingredients:

- 6-8 chicken pieces (your choice)
- 1 1/2 cups of flour
- 2/3 cup of milk
- 2-3 eggs
- 1 packet of dried tomato soup mix
- 1 packet of powdered Italian dressing
- Vegetable oil
- Salt
- Black pepper

Preparation:

1. Beat the eggs in a bowl, add the milk, and blend.
2. Make a dry mix of the Italian dressing, soup mix, flour, and black pepper.
3. Dip the chicken pieces in the flour mixture, ensuring that all portions become coated properly.

4. Place the chicken pieces in a skillet and fry them on a medium heat (350F).
5. Leave the pieces in the skillet for about half an hour. Turn them occasionally to get an even fry.
6. After removing the pieces from the skillet, place them in a kitchen cloth to remove excess oil.

This KFC-style fried chicken can be served with gravy or mashed potatoes to bring in added taste.

Dennis Wayne Bagwell

If you were allowed to choose one last meal before you were to take your last breath, what would you choose that meal to be? A steak? Fried chicken, maybe? Perhaps a burger and fries? For one convicted murderer, the answer would be "all of the above" - and then some.

Dennis Wayne Bagwell grew up in Texas and had a history of assaultive behavior, threats of violence against others, and parole violations, having served thirteen years of an eighteen year sentence for the crime of attempted capital murder. Before that conviction, he had at one time also been charged with misdemeanor assault.

Out of prison and on parole in September of 1995, Bagwell and his girlfriend were living in a small camping trailer on some property that belonged to his mother and stepfather. At some point, Bagwell's mother and stepfather decided the arrangement was not working out and his mother told Bagwell that he and his girlfriend would have to leave. Bagwell and his girlfriend moved in with friends in a neighboring town, but on September 20, they returned to his mother's home, allegedly to borrow some money. While his girlfriend was in the travel trailer, supposedly due to not feeling well, Bagwell confronted his mother in the mobile home she shared with her husband, her husband's granddaughter, and Bagwell's half-sister and niece.

After telling his girlfriend that his mother would give him only $20.00, he returned to his mother's house. While the girlfriend remained in the travel trailer, she later told authorities that she saw Bagwell hit his mother. She also heard screams and other sounds from the other three occupants of the house - Bagwell's half-sister and a 14-year-old girl, his stepfather's granddaughter, who was also raped. Also killed was the 4-year-old daughter of his half-sister, who was brutally beaten and her skull crushed. The bodies of the four victims were discovered by Bagwell's stepfather when he returned home from work that afternoon.

Dennis Wayne Bagwell was arrested and charged with their murders that same day. (In addition to the murders that took place on September 20 of that year, it was later proven that Bagwell had also killed an elderly man two weeks earlier by kicking him to death. He was tried for that crime and given life in prison.) A little over thirteen months after the murders of his mother and three other family members, on November 1, 1996, Dennis Wayne Bagwell was found guilty of those murders; on November 7, 1996, Bagwell was ordered to be put to death.

Bagwell appealed his conviction, which was later upheld by the Texas Court of Criminal Appeals. He continued to file further appeals and reliefs, all of which were denied; the final appeal denial took place on November 14, 2004, a little over nine years after the murders. His date of execution by lethal injection was scheduled for February 17, 2005.

So, what does someone who has brutally murdered four family members, two of them children, and an elderly man, choose for his last meal here on earth? Well, apparently Bagwell's appetite was as large as his humanity and compassion were small, because he requested a steak, fried chicken, onion rings, French fries, two hamburgers, barbecued ribs, scrambled eggs, bacon, salad, coffee, iced tea, and milk - and, for dessert, peach cobbler. There is no word on if he finished it all.

Dennis Wayne Bagwell's Peach Cobbler

Ingredients:

- 1/2 cup unsalted butter, melted
- 1 cup all-purpose flour
- 2 cups brown or white sugar, separated
- 3 teaspoons baking powder
- A pinch of salt
- 1 cup milk (do not use skim milk)
- 5-6 medium peaches
- 2 teaspoons ground cinnamon
- 1 teaspoon vanilla extract
- 1 tablespoon fresh lemon juice

Directions:

1. Preheat oven to 375 degrees F.
2. Peel and pit the peaches, then thinly slice them.
3. Pour 1/2 cup of butter into the baking dish.

4. In a bowl, mix the flour, 1 cup of the sugar, baking powder, and a pinch of salt.
5. Stir the milk into the dry ingredients to make a batter.
6. Mix until just combined.
7. Pour the batter into the baking dish. The batter and butter will not fully mix, which is fine--this will make a tender cobbler.
8. In the small pan or pot, combine the sliced peaches, the lemon juice, and the other cup of sugar.
9. Bring this mixture to a boil, stirring constantly.
10. Remove the peaches from the heat and add the vanilla extract, stirring to combine.
11. Pour the peach mixture over the batter. Again, some peaches will sink in, but the two mixtures will not fully combine.
12. Sprinkle the top with cinnamon.
13. Put the dish in the middle rack of the oven and bake until the top is golden brown, about 40-45 minutes.
14. Cobbler may be served warm or at room temperature.

Ronnie Lee Gardner

Ronnie Lee Gardner was born on January 16, 1961 and was convicted of murder and executed for his crimes in 2010. Gardner's prolonged incarceration of 25 years sparked controversy, and ultimately prompted the House of Representatives to try to create new laws limiting the number of appeals that a capital case could have. The legislation, though, failed to become law.

Back in October of 1984, Gardner committed a robbery in Salt Lake City, and shot Melvyn John Otterstrom in the process. However, this crime was not what got him the death sentence. Gardner attempted to escape from custody when transported to court for the shooting of Otterstrom. During this unsuccessful escape attempt, he shot and killed attorney Michael Burdell. In fact, Gardner was convicted of both counts of murder and attempted escape. For the murder of Melvyn Otterstrom he was sentenced to life imprisonment and for the murder of Michael Burdell he was sentenced to death.

Despite being convicted of both counts of murder, Gardner filed countless appeals to his conviction seeking to overturn these convictions or commute the sentence to life in prison. After families of the victims testified, his death sentence was upheld in 2010.

The execution of Gardner was notable because it was carried out by firing squad, the first of its kind in the U.S. Gardner said he chose death by firing squad because of his Mormon background. In fact, shortly before his execution he sought the guidance of Mormon priest to atone for "sins" associated with the murders he committed.

The day of his execution, Gardner walked voluntarily to his place of execution and did not say he had any last words, and responded "I do not, no." On June 18, 2010, Gardner was executed by firing squad at the Utah State Prison in Draper. Gardner was executed in Utah for his crimes and was the first to be executed by firing squad since Gary Gilmore.

Utah is the only state in the United States that allows execution by firing squad in addition to lethal injection as an option. Like many states, the Utah penitentiary system grants its condemned inmates a last meal request. Gardner, for his final meal, requested a meal of steak, lobster tail, a dessert of apple pie and vanilla ice cream, and washed it down with 7-Up forty eight hours before his scheduled execution. He requested his last meal forty-eight hours in advance because he wanted to undergo a fast before his execution, which he completed.

Ronnie Lee Gardner's Apple Pie

Ingredients:

- 3/4 cup of butter
- 4 tbsp. cold water
- 2 cups of flour filling
- 6 apples
- 2 tbsp. cornstarch butter
- 3/4 cup sugar
- 1 tsp. cinnamon

Preparation
1. Cut up butter and flour.
2. Add water.
3. Roll into a ball.
4. Cut in half.
5. Roll out with a pin.
6. Line pie tin with dough.
7. Peel, core and slice apples.
8. Mix in bowl the sugar, cornstarch, and cinnamon.
9. Sprinkle the apples over the mixture.
10. Put the butter on top.
11. Put the top crust on.
12. Baste the crust with melted butter.
13. Cook at 350 degrees for one hour.
14. Cover loosely with foil for the first 40 minutes.

This recipe makes 6 to 8 servings.

John William Elliot

Death row inmate John Williams Elliot ordered one cup of hot tea and six chocolate chip cookies for his last meal. He was executed on the evening of February 4, 2003 for the rape and murder of Joyce Munguia. The execution was by lethal injection and took place in Huntsville, Texas. Elliot was the 828th murderer executed in the U.S. since 1976 and the 296th murderer executed in Texas since 1976.

Elliot was born on March 25, 1960. Elliot had a prior history of other crimes including burglary, illegal possession of weapons, and disorderly conduct. In 1984 he was convicted for an attempted burglary crime and was given 10 years of probation. On June 13, 1986 he raped and beat to death Joyce Munguia in Austin, Texas. He was sentenced on January 15, 1987. Elliot had two accomplices, Ricky Elizondo and Pete Ramirez, who also raped Munguia at the crime scene. Elizondo was sentenced to 10 years and Ramirez was sentenced to 15 years.

Elliot's victim, Joyce Munguia, was an 18-year-old mother of a one-year-old toddler. In June 1996, Munguia was waiting for a bus when she was observed by Daniel Hansen. She was invited by Hansen to join him and a number of men that included John William Elliot, Pete Ramirez, and Ricky Elizondo. Munguia conversed with the men and consumed beer and cocaine. She became drunk and Hansen walked her home. Elliot followed them, accompanied by Elizondo and Ramirez. Elliot carried Munguia to a wood under a railroad track bridge. Here she was gang raped by Elliot, Ramirez, and Elizondo. Afterwards Elliot beat Munguia and killed her with a metal motorcycle chain. She was struck 16 times on her head and 8 times on the face.

After being sentenced on January 15, 1987 for the rape and murder of Munguia, the court set Elliot's execution for August 24, 1994. On August 2, 1994, though, Elliot requested to stay his execution and the federal district court approved his execution stay on August 5, 1994. In September of 1999 Elliot was denied relief by both the state and federal court. In October of 2002 the court set a second order of execution. On February 4, 2003, after enjoying his last meal, Elliot was finally executed for the crimes he committed against Munguia.

John William Elliot's Chocolate Chip Cookies

The secret to perfectly soft homemade chocolate chip cookies is cornstarch (this is part of the reason that cookie recipes that include pudding mix are soft). It doesn't take that much, just a couple of teaspoons.

Ingredients:

- 1 1/2 cups all-purpose flour
- 2 teaspoons of cornstarch
- 1 teaspoon of baking soda
- 1/2 teaspoon kosher salt
- 1/2 cup (1 stick) of unsalted butter
- Softened 3/4 cup light brown sugar
- Packed 1/4 cup granulated sugar
- 1 large egg
- 1 teaspoon of vanilla
- 1 1/2 cups of semi-sweet chocolate chips

Directions

1. Mix flour, cornstarch, baking soda, and salt together and set aside.
2. Beat butter and both sugars together with a mixer until light and fluffy.
3. Add the egg and vanilla and mix until fully incorporated.
4. Add in the flour mixture until combined.

5. Mix in the chocolate chips until evenly distributed throughout the dough.
6. Chill the dough for about an hour (this will keep the cookies from spreading as much as they bake).
7. Preheat oven to 350 degrees Fahrenheit and line cookie sheets* with parchment paper.
8. Form the dough into balls (about 1 inch for smaller cookies and about 1 1/2 inches for larger ones) and place on the lined cookie sheets.
9. Bake 8-10 minutes for the smaller cookies and 10-12 minutes for the larger ones. A shorter baking time yields a softer cookie.
10. Cool on the cookie sheets for 10 minutes and then place cookies on a cooling rack (the completely cooled cookies are delicious, but the warm cookies are particularly excellent).

Makes about 40 smaller cookies or 24 larger cookies. *If only using one cookie sheet, place cookie dough in the refrigerator while the first batch is baking and make sure the cookie sheet is completely cooled down before placing chilled dough on it.

Gary Leon Brown

Gary Leon Brown was born on July 14, 1958 in Birmingham, AL. He had a history of substance abuse that began his junior high school years. Brown never seemed to turn his life around and get back on track. Brown met his wife while he was in prison on Death Row.

On May 26, 1996, Brown and several other men went on a fishing trip. During the trip they consumed alcohol. Afterwards, they went to a lounge and continued to consume alcohol while plotting to visit victim Jack McGraw. They wanted to visit the victim, get him drunk, and once he passed out they would rob him.

Upon leaving the lounge they began to execute their plan. However, their plan changed once they arrived and McGraw stated that he could not drink with them. He had to work the next day, and did not feel like partying. McGraw followed the men to their car, and they attacked him. They decided to kill McGraw and proceed with the robbery.

Brown was convicted of stabbing McGraw in the back with a pocketknife over 59 times. The victim's body had approximately 78 stab wounds. After the brutal stabbing, the victim's body was left in his mobile home lifeless. The victim's body was later discovered by a neighborhood child. Brown and his accomplices partook in this senseless crime and made away with only a few appliances and $67. He admitted to his part in the death and was arrested on June 5, 1996. Brown was later charged with capital murder and sentenced to life in prison.

There was a lot of controversy surrounding this crime. The victim was a homosexual male and many wanted to rule it as a hate crime. However, it was never declared a hate crime. This is the only known crime that Brown has committed.

He spent a total of 16 years on death row in the Holman Prison in Atmore, Alabama. Brown made great use of his time while in prison and was frequently visited by family members. He was known for his religious aspects of life before and during his prison sentence. Brown could often be seen praying and singing spiritual hymns with his visitors. Also, Brown had never missed a service since Monday night church service began in 1989. He was counseled by a former prison chaplain during his prison term. The chaplain later testified at his clemency hearing.

On his final day Brown gave his wife several items such as bibles and money from his commissary. He gave his son a watch and wooden cross. The remainders of his personal items were distributed amongst his death row mates.

Brown was executed on April 23, 2003 by lethal injection. He was 44 years old when he was executed. After a series of injections, Brown was pronounced dead at 6:19 p.m. His wife was present during the execution, and stood only a few feet away from the witness room. They communicated briefly before he passed away.

Most prisoners choose to have a plentiful and well thought out last meal. However, Gary did not have a last meal request. Instead he chose to eat an ice cream sandwich from a vending machine inside of the prison.

Gary Leon Brown's Ice Cream Sandwich

An ice cream sandwich can be an ideal recipe to prepare at home during any time of the year. Be it mint, vanilla or chocolate cake, the taste remains great in any ice cream sandwich that's made at home. So, don't waste time to taste the best of recipes!

Ingredients:

- 1/2 cup of butter
- 1/2 cup of sugar (granulated)
- 1 large egg
- 1 teaspoon of vanilla extract
- 1/2 cup of flour
- 4 cups of ice cream
- Pinch of salt

Preparation:

1. Preheat the oven at 350 F.
2. Prepare a pan by spraying it with a non-stick vegetable spray and lining it with a baking sheet.
3. Melt butter in another pan and stir.
4. Put the butter in a bowl and add the sugar. Whisk.
5. Add the egg and vanilla extract. Whisk again.
6. Adding the flour and salt and stir until smooth.
7. Spread this batter evenly in the pan you prepared earlier.
8. Bake it for about 10 minutes or until the cake is dry.

9. Allow the cake to cool after removing it from the oven.
10. After putting half of the cake on a cutting board, cut it crosswise.
11. Spread the ice cream on top of the first sheet, then place the second sheet on the ice cream.
12. Wrap the cake tightly in plastic wrap and leave it in the refrigerator for a few hours.
13. Cut the cake into square or rectangle pieces and serve.
14. If there are any leftovers, you can store them in the freezer for a week.

James David Autry

James David Autry was born on September 27, 1954 and had a lengthy criminal record after turning 18. While Autry worked primarily as a day laborer and drifter, he was convicted of assault and attempted robbery in 1972 and was sentenced to five years in prison.

Paroled after three years, Autry violated parole by committing another burglary in 1975, and he was subsequently sentenced to eight years in prison. It was five years later that Autry would commit the murders and attempted murder that would give him the death penalty.

On April 20, 1980, Autry and his co-defendant and roommate John Alton Sandifer robbed a convenience store. During the robbery, Autry shot the convenience store clerk with a handgun and proceeded to shoot two witnesses. One of the witnesses, Reverend Joe Broussard, died instantly, while the other, a Greek seaman named Anthanasios Svarnas, survived but was permanently disabled.

The gunmen did not take any money during the failed robbery attempt, although a carton of beer was missing during the initial investigation.

Autry was scheduled to die by lethal injection in 1983 but was given a stay of execution 31 minutes prior to his execution by Justice Byron White. Autry also sued to have his execution televised, but the Texas Board of Corrections denied his request. During his appeals, Autry argued that his punishment was unfairly reached given that other, similar crimes did not lead to a death sentence. He also stated that it was his accomplice who was responsible for the shootings, although his accomplice was given a plea bargain to cooperate.

With his appeals denied, Autry was executed in 1984, less than three years after his conviction. Texas is known to give their condemned prisoners both a last meal and the ability to state any final words before the actual execution. Autry did not give any statement or final words before being executed. However, he opted for a final meal that was rather plain and generic to some. Autry requested a hamburger, French fries, and a Dr. Pepper.

James David Autry's Burger

Homemade burgers are easy and quick to make, and are perfect for any night of the week. Making burgers at home rather than going to a fast food joint can save you a ton of money as well.

Obviously the key ingredient in a burger is the patty. For beef patties, you will want to purchase lean ground beef. A lot of people follow the 80/20 percent lean fat rule when buying ground beef. You can also use ground turkey to make the burger healthier. When it comes to toppings, there are endless possibilities. You can do the standard mustard, lettuce, tomatoes, onions, pickles etc., or you can go with mushrooms, jalapenos, cheeses, avocado, hot sauces, bacon. The options are endless when it comes to what you can put on a burger and by making them at home you can have tons of fun experimenting with different toppings. You will also need hamburger buns, which are easy to find at grocery stores.

Ingredients:

- 1 pound of ground beef (for 4 patties)
- 1 egg
- 1/2 a teaspoon of black pepper
- 4 hamburger buns

Preparation:

1. Preheat grill to a high heat.

2. Whisk together the egg with the salt and pepper in a bowl.
3. Add the beef and blend by hand.
4. Make patties that around 1-inch thick.
5. Place them on the grill and cook for around 7 minutes, or to taste.

Place the burgers on the buns and garnish if desired

Philip Workman

Philip Workman was born on June 1, 1953 and was a death row inmate in Tennessee. He murdered a police officer following a robbery attempt in Memphis, and was convicted in 1982. The underlying facts of Workman's case, though, remain controversial and questionable.

In 1981, Workman was living with his wife and daughter in Columbus, Georgia and was addicted to cocaine. He would hitchhike to Memphis, Tennessee, where on August 5, 1981 he robbed a Wendy's fast food restaurant with a handgun. During the robbery, an employee triggered a silent alarm and three Memphis police officers responded to the alarm. Workman would subsequently kill Lt. Ronald Oliver during the crime, and it was for this crime he would be sentenced to be put to death by a Memphis jury.

However, the post-trial reports after the death sentence was rendered would be the reason for controversy and media scrutiny. Five of the jurors who had convicted Workman signed affidavits declaring they no longer believed in the verdict or the sentence, citing medical and ballistic evidence that was unheard during the actual trial. The jurors claimed that the lack of mitigating evidence would have swayed their opinion of guilt and sentence if heard in court. Additional evidence that was inconsistent was the ballistic evidence cited. The evidence suggested that the fatal shot did not match that of Workman's gun and it has been suggested that the fatal shot was actually from one of the officer's firearms, not Workman.

The U.S. Supreme Court refused to hear any appeals of his case, which ended his potential appeals. Workman was convicted and sentenced to death in Tennessee. Workman's last meal request was both highly unusual and was rejected by the Tennessee authorities, once again leading to media coverage. Workman requested, as his last meal, to decline a meal for himself and instead deliver a vegetarian pizza to a local homeless shelter. His request was summarily denied by the Tennessee authorities, which led to media coverage across the country. In light of the media coverage, a number of homeless shelters in the area received hundreds of pizzas donated by those following the case.

Philip Workman, despite the media attention and celebrity advocacy, was executed by lethal injection on May 9, 2007. Workman did not have any last words during his execution.

Philip Workman's Vegetarian Pizza

Pizzas with interesting toppings are a common favorite among fast food lovers. Vegetarian pizza, in particular, has so many takers for the unique taste it delivers. From making the vegetarian pizza base to preparing the sauce, and finally assembling the pizza itself, the entire process seems to be ideally suited for home cooking.

Ingredients for pizza base:

- 3 cups of flour
- 1 cup of water (warm)
- 2 teaspoons of yeast
- 1/4 teaspoon of sugar
- Olive oil
- 1/2 teaspoon of salt

Preparation:

1. After dissolving the sugar in warm water, add yeast and stir the mix. In around 15 minutes, the yeast will double in size.
2. Mix the flour and salt separately and pour in olive oil.
3. Put the frothy yeast mixture into the bowl containing the flour, and stir the mix till it turns sticky.
4. Keep adding flour as you stir the mixture.
5. Knead the dough to make it smooth. You can dust it with flour so that it doesn't remain sticky.

6. After adding some olive oil, leave the dough in a covered bowl.
7. Keep the dough in the refrigerator for an hour or so.

Ingredients for pizza sauce and toppings:

- 5 tomatoes
- 3 garlic
- 1 capsicum
- 2 tablespoons of olive oil
- 2 tablespoons of basil
- 1 tablespoon of oregano
- Crushed herbs
- Black pepper
- Salt
- Olives
- Grated Mozzarella cheese (to taste)

Preparation:

1. After frying the garlic in a pan, add the chopped tomatoes and stir for about 5 minutes.
2. Slice the onion and capsicum after the tomatoes simmer.
3. Marinate the veggies with olive oil, basil, and oregano for about 15 minutes.
4. Add herbs, salt and crushed pepper to the tomatoes.

Assembling the vegetarian pizza:

1. Now make the dough into a large ball, or two medium-sized ones.
2. Preheat oven to 200 F, grease the pan with olive oil, and dust with flour.
3. After flattening the dough into a disk, roll the dough balls on a floured surface, starting from the center to outer edges.
4. Gently place the pizza base in the baking pan, after brushing the area with oil.
5. Now it's time to spread the tomato sauce on the pizza.
6. After topping with olives and veggies, sprinkle on the pizza cheese.
7. Bake the pizza in the oven for about 15 minutes, or until the base turns golden brown.

Your favorite vegetarian pizza is all ready for serving!

Karla Faye Tucker

Karla Faye Tucker was born on November 18, 1959 and was the first woman to be executed in the United States since 1984, and the first in Texas since 1863. She was convicted of murder in Texas in 1984 but was not put on death row until fourteen years later. Her gender and conversion to Christianity inspired a movement to commute her sentence and show leniency to a "reformed" and "rehabilitated" criminal. This movement included many civil liberties groups, clergy, human rights activists, and even foreign government officials. However, these petitions failed to commute her sentence and she was executed by lethal injection on February 3, 1998 for her crimes.

Tucker was born and raised in Houston, Texas and lived a troubled childhood. The marriage of her parents was rocky, and Tucker started smoking and doing drugs at the age of 12. When she was 14, she dropped out of school and followed her mother to be a rock groupie and turned to prostitution to survive. In fact, she began traveling with notable bands like The Allman Brothers Band, The Marshall Tucker Band, and the Eagles.

She was married at age 16 to a mechanic, but that marriage dissolved soon after. In her 20's she met and began hanging out with a biker gang, and it was in this situation she would soon find herself convicted of murder.

Tucker was charged with murdering her boyfriend Danny Garret's friend Jerry Dean after a drug fueled night. The motive for Tucker's crime was burglary, since she needed money to feed her drug habit. Both Danny and Karla were arrested and charged with the murder of Dean.

In 1983, Karla and Danny were indicted and tried separately for the murders. Although Karla was found guilty, the death penalty was rarely sought for female defendants but due to the heinous crime she was sentenced to death in 1984 (along with her boyfriend Danny, who would die from liver disease in 1993). Her requests for retrials and appeals were denied, as was her appeal for clemency (She claimed she was under the influence of drugs and could not have committed the crimes had she not taken drugs). After her appeals were denied, she was executed by lethal injection on February 2, 1998.

The night of her execution, Tucker's last meal request of a banana, a peach, and a garden salad with ranch dressing was granted. Unlike most condemned criminals, Tucker's last meal was not overly ostentatious, and in fact, is considered unique since most condemned prisoners request meals of steak, seafood, or fried chicken with cake or ice cream.

Karla Faye Tucker's Garden Salad

The key to the perfect garden salad is the freshness of vegetables. The base of the salad is typically lettuce or spinach. There are many varieties of lettuce to choose from, from iceberg to romaine. Kale can also make a good green salad.

After you choose your leafy green base, the possibilities are endless. Typical garden salad ingredients are cucumbers, tomatoes, bell peppers, carrots, radish, and onions. You can also add fresh mushrooms, sprouts, olives, snow peas, cauliflower, broccoli, and hot peppers.

If you want to add protein, grilled chicken is perfect along with diced turkey, ham, bacon crumbles and boiled egg. Standard cheddar cheese or blue cheese crumbles are popular cheese choices.

Ingredients:

- 2 tomatoes
- 1 lettuce
- 1/2 cucumber
- 1 green onion
- 1/4 cup of Vinaigrette
- Salt
- Pepper

1. Cut the tomatoes into small segments.

2. Slice and chop the other vegetables, and place all the ingredients in a bowl.
3. Add salt and pepper to taste.

Gary Mark Gilmore

Unlike most people sentenced to death, Gary Mark Gilmore wanted nothing to do with appeals or with prolonging his life. He was ready to die from the moment he was convicted and sentenced to death, even going against those who were trying to make appeals. In fact, Gilmore fired three attorneys during his trial. In addition, he attempted suicide on two separate occasions during his incarceration. He also went on a hunger strike in attempts to end his life sooner.

Gilmore spent only six months in prison before his execution took place. He was asked whether he wanted to die by firing squad or by hanging, to which he replied that he wanted to be shot. Gilmore's wishes would finally be granted when he was executed January 17, 1977. Liquor was smuggled into the prison the prior evening, and Gilmore enjoyed a farewell party of his own.

Gilmore began a life of crime at an early age. It was at the age of 15 that he started committing various petty thefts and other crimes. It ran in the family, though, as Gilmore's father had families in many different areas and himself was a conman. Gilmore would spend several years in prison for armed robbery, and would be transferred from his original housing unit to another state prison because of his violent behavior. He was diagnosed with antisocial personality disorder while serving his 15-year sentence.

After his release, he moved to Utah to live with a cousin. This is also where he began a relationship with a 19-year old female and ultimately committed murder. He first killed a gas station attendant during a robbery, and the following night he would kill the manager of a Provo motel. After the murders Gilmore shot himself as he attempted to discard the gun. An eyewitness saw him attempting to hide the gun in bushes. The witness had also recently heard about the murders on the scanner, and seeing the blood on Gilmore's hand, phoned the local police department.

Gilmore's trial lasted only two days. On October 7, 1976 he was convicted of the first murder, for which he was sentenced to die. He was never charged with the second murder, although he did confess to it. Gilmore's last words were 'Let's do it.' It has become an urban legend that this is where Nike developed their motto 'Just Do it.' January 17, 1977, Gilmore was shot to death by firing squad, and pronounced dead at 8:07 a.m.

Gilmore reportedly requested a last meal of steak, potatoes, milk, and coffee. However, Gilmore only drank the milk and coffee and left the steak and potatoes.

Gary Gilmore's Steak and Potatoes

Ingredients:

- Cut of steak of your choice
- 2 small red potatoes per person, cut in half
- 1 tbsp. of butter per steak
- 1 tbsp. of butter per potato
- Olive oil
- Canola oil
- Pinch of salt
- Pinch of pepper
- Pinch of garlic powder

Preparation:

1. Preheat the oven to 450 degrees.
2. Put the halved potatoes in a baking dish and drizzle with olive oil. Liberally shake salt, pepper, and garlic powder over potatoes. Bake for about 40 minutes until potatoes are tender.
3. About 30 minutes into the cooking time of the potatoes, coat a pan with canola oil over high heat.
4. Place salted steaks in the pan. Prepare to flip several times to allow the steaks to cook evenly.
5. Just before the steaks are cooked to your preference*, add butter and pepper.
6. Remove potatoes from oven and test for softness.
7. Put butter on top of potatoes to melt.

8. Plate your steak and potatoes and enjoy!

A food thermometer can help test doneness as follows:

- *120° F (48.8° C) = Rare*
- *130° F (54.4° C) = Medium rare*
- *140° F (60° C) = Medium*
- *150° F (65.5° C) = Medium well*
- *160° F (71.1° C) = Well done*

Desmond Keith Carter

Desmond Carter was only thirty-five years old at the time of his death. Carter had been convicted in the stabbing death of an elderly woman. According to prosecutors, Carter stabbed Helen Purdy thirteen times in an attempted robbery. The two individuals were neighbors. Carter had stab wounds on his leg, a criminal record, and a recent history of instability.

Carter chose to forego the usual last meal and did not make a special request. Instead he chose to eat at the prison cantina. In what was perhaps a show of defiance, he paid for his final meal out of his prison account. He paid $4.20 for two cheeseburgers, a steak sub sandwich, and two cokes. After his meal, he waited for the 2:00 am appointed time for the execution. At the event, he mouthed, "I love you, Pop," to his father. Officials read a written statement apologizing to the victim and her family. Carter was pronounced dead less than twenty minutes later.

In the months leading up to the victim's murder, Carter's mother had grown concerned about her son's mental health and tried to seek help at nearby hospitals, but the family was uninsured and they were turned away. Carter also had a drug addiction problem. On the day of the crime, he claimed he was high on alcohol, crack cocaine, and tranquilizers. He said that he went to his neighbor, Purdy, to borrow money to buy cocaine. She was initially skeptical, but agreed to loan him five dollars. After she changed her mind, a fight ensued. Purdy was stabbed nineteen times, and died.

Carter had initially confessed to the crime, saying that the two had fought and Purdy had fell on the knife. He later changed his story, and admitted stabbing her.

Carter had a long history of substance abuse dating as far back as his teenage years. According to accounts, he had a difficult childhood and turned to violence and drugs at a young age. Before the murder, Carter was already a convicted felon. He had served four years of a twelve-year sentence in New York State for which he had been convicted of abduction. He had to get permission from the parole system to leave the state and move to North Carolina to be close to his family. There, he lived with his mother.

Carter has been cited as a case where the system did not work. He was unable to get help despite his family seeking it. He had a history of violent crime, which showed itself in the Purdy crime.

His last meal reflects the way Carter lived his life. Two cheeseburgers, one steak sub, two coca-colas, all purchased from the prison canteen with his own earned money.

Desmond Keith Carter's Cheeseburgers

For those who are keen on recipes that don't take more than 5 to 10 minutes to cook, cheeseburgers serve as the perfect answer. While it takes very little time to prepare cheeseburgers, the ultimate taste is matchless. And finally when you serve the burgers on buns, you realize that there can't be a better combination for your loved ones at home.

Ingredients:

- 1 pound of ground beef (makes 4 burgers)
- 4 American cheese singles
- 4 burger buns
- 1 tablespoon of Worcestershire sauce
- 1/2 a teaspoon of onion powder
- 1/2 a teaspoon of garlic powder
- Salt

Preparation:

- Mix the ground beef, Worcestershire sauce, and seasonings in a bowl.
- Divide the mixture into 4 patties of equal size and around 3/4 inches in width.
- Cook the patties for five minutes a side on a medium-high heated grill.
- Place the cheese on the burgers about a minute ahead of removing them from the grill.

- Serve in the burger bugs.

And that's all; your cheeseburgers are ready for serving! You can also top them with either ketchup or pickles to offer extra taste.

Ruth Brown Snyder

Ruth Snyder was born March 27, 1895, and lived until she met her death at the Sing Sing Prison on January 12, 1928. Snyder was convicted of killing her husband, Albert, in 1927. She was executed in the electric chair as punishment for her crime. There are photographs of the Snyder electrocution today thanks to Tom Howard, a journalist allowed to witness the execution. While Sing Sing did not allow cameras to be taken into the prison, he taped a miniature camera to his ankle, snapping a photo at the moment Snyder took her final breath.

The details of the crime are well documented. In 1925, Snyder was a housewife in Queens, New York and had an affair with a married corset salesman, Henry Gray. Gray and Snyder soon conspired to murder her current husband, since Snyder was very indifferent towards him. During the course of the planning, Snyder managed to get her husband to buy life insurance in the amount of $48,000 (as a brief aside, she convinced the insurance agent to double the policy fraudulently, which led to the insurance agent's conviction and prison sentence).

With the policy in place, Snyder tried to kill her husband seven times, and failed each of the seven times. On the eighth attempt, on March 20, 1927, Snyder suffocated her husband with rags soaked in chloroform and then staged a burglary. Detectives were skeptical, since there was poor evidence of a burglary and break in. The police broke the conspiracy when they found property Snyder claimed was stolen hidden in the house. Knowing that the burglary was a smokescreen, the police suspected Snyder was the murderer and she was promptly arrested.

Snyder's trial was prompt but was heavily covered by the media. In fact, the media dubbed the murder "the dumb-belle murder case" because the planning and implementation of the conspiracy was so poorly executed. Snyder was convicted of her crime and sent to death row, where she became the first woman to be executed at Sing Sing since 1899.

The notoriety of the case and the resulting filming of her execution were groundbreaking. Photographs of Snyder strapped to the electric chair while the electric current was running through her body was the first time a person was filmed and photographed while being executed. In fact, the camera used to photograph Snyder's death is part of the Smithsonian National Museum of American History's permanent collection.

Snyder was given a last meal of unknown content, but some speculate that it was a simple meal of chicken, rice, and red velvet cake. However, these are just speculation and there are no documented articles or photos on what she ate.

Ruth Snyder's Red Velvet Cake

Ingredients:

- 3 cups of all-purpose flour
- 2 cups of granulated sugar
- 1/4 cup of unsweetened cocoa powder
- 2 tsp. of baking soda
- 1 tsp. of salt
- 2 cups of plain non-dairy milk
- 1 cup of vegetable oil
- 3 tablespoons of vanilla extract
- 2 tablespoons of white vinegar
- 1/4 cup red food coloring
- 1/4 cup beet juice

Preparation:

1. Preheat oven at 350 degrees.
2. Oil two 8" round baking pans. Then, in a large bowl, stir together the dry ingredients: flour, sugar, cocoa powder, baking soda, and salt.
3. Add the non-dairy milk, oil, food coloring (or beet juice), and vanilla to the dry ingredients, and stir together until it's just blended.
4. Add the vinegar and stir briefly.
5. Pour the batter right away into prepared pans and bake in the warmed oven for 35-50 minutes.

6. If a toothpick comes out clean then the cake is done. If not, then cook for 5-10 minutes longer.
7. Cool in the pans for about 10 minutes.
8. Gently take cake out of the pans, and let the cake cool completely on wire racks.

Joseph Mitchell "Yogi" Parsons

Joseph Mitchell "Yogi" Parsons was notable for a variety of unsavory criminal acts. He was a fugitive when he stabbed 30-year-old Richard Lynn Ernest nine times, resulting in his death. He later alleged that Ernest made a homosexual advance to him after he hitched a ride with him in California. He is also the last person to have met his maker by lethal injection in Utah.

Parsons' father was in jail when he was born. After a dismal few years of poverty, his mother moved him and his sister to Florida where she married a man well versed in child abuse. This dysfunctional family resulted in beatings and a variety of sordid abuse. His sister had similar issues. She introduced her young brother to a drug dealer who so impressed Parsons that he tattooed his name, Yogi, on his arm.

With three burglary convictions, no ability to make money and only a drug dealer as an idol, Parsons went in search of his biological father in New York. His father rejected him, and Parsons was truly alone. His next venture was Las Vegas where he was befriended by David Wood, another deviant. Shortly after, on the hunt for marijuana with Wood, he pointed a 22-caliber revolver at a cab driver and stole his cab. He spent five years in a Nevada prison for this.

Parsons struggled with identity issues. After murdering Ernest and being in possession of his car and credit cards, he maintained that he actually was Ernest. The Yogi tattoo on his arm was the name of another man. His last incarnation, on death row, was as the "Rainbow Warrior."

While he was a career criminal, starting with three burglary convictions while he was still a minor in Florida, his criminal status was not enough to elevate him to heights achieved by more notorious killers. His fame is based on his last meal in prison. He shared his last meal of Whoppers, French fries, chocolate chip ice cream, a chocolate shake, and Hubba Bubba bubblegum with his brother and cousin.

"Yogi" Parsons Whopper-Style Burgers

What sets Burger King Whoppers apart from any other fast food joint's burger is that they are flame broiled. In order to achieve a similar taste at home you will need to use a grill or broiler.

The first step is to buy decent ground beef to make into patties, or you can buy patties already formed to save time. The patty should be a little bit bigger than the bun you are using.

Season the patties with some salt and pepper, and place on a grill flame or broiler. Cook until done, or to your preference.

The typical whopper from Burger King has mayonnaise, ketchup, lettuce, tomatoes, dill pickles, and onions. However, you can add cheese, jalapenos, bacon, or other toppings of your choice.

Ingredients:

- 1/4 pound of ground beef
- 1 sesame seed bun
- 3 dill pickles (sliced)
- 3 onion rings
- 2 slices of tomato
- 1 tablespoon of mayonnaise
- Salt
- 1 teaspoon of catsup

Preparation:

1. Prepare the above ingredients.
2. Toast the sesame seed bun lightly in a skillet.
3. Make the ground beef into a patty.
4. Add salt.
5. Cook on the grill for 2-3 minutes.
6. Flip the patty and cook for a further 2-3 minutes.
7. Assemble the ingredients within the bun with the hamburger, and serve.

Ricky Ray Rector

There it sat. Like a normal meal. Steak, fried chicken, cherry Kool-Aid and pecan pie. That's what Ricky Ray Rector ordered from death row before being lethally injected in Arkansas in 1992. Whether Rector really knew what he was doing when he ordered the meal will forever be debated.

The fateful story began on March 21, 1981. Rector and some friends headed to Tommy's Old-Fashioned Home-Style Restaurant in Conway to go dancing. Instead, they would leave with their lives changed forever, all over a $3 cover charge. One of Rector's friends couldn't pay the cover, and that was an issue. They weren't allowed in, and the conversation with the bouncer grew heated. Instead of it ending there, however, it turned ugly. Rector pulled out his .38 handgun and began firing. The shots hit three men, killing Arthur Criswell. The other two recovered, but Criswell died instantly, and Rector went on the run.

For three days, he hid out. He was in the woods, he was at friends' homes, and he was anywhere the cops couldn't find him. Eventually, the cops were at Rector's mother's home and Rector showed up. There was discussion, and Officer Robert Martin turned to speak with Rector's mother. That would be Martin's final mistake. Rector shot the officer twice, before presumably heading on the run again.

Upon being captured again, Rector saw no way out. He turned the gun on himself and, right near his temple, fired. Like his final meal, however, the suicide attempt remained unfinished. He had blasted off his frontal lobe, essentially giving himself a lobotomy, but remained alive.

He was later tested, with his I.Q. falling under 70, making him categorized as mentally retarded. No matter how much his lawyers argued that the retardation was reason enough to not execute Rector, it fell on deaf ears as Judge George F. Hartje ruled he was competent to stand trial. Rector had killed a cop, and a doorman, and he would have to pay.

This was 1992, and Bill Clinton was being called soft. So he decided to go back to his home state and show he wasn't, encouraging the execution to go on as scheduled. Ten years later, the Supreme Court would ban the execution of people with mental retardation. But then, it was legal, and Rector chowed down on his final meal, eating the steak and fried chicken, washing it down with the Kool-Aid. But there, he decided he was finished, apparently not realizing what was about to occur. Instead, he pushed the pecan pie to the side. "I'll save it for later," he told the guards.

Ricky Ray Rector's Pecan Pie

Ingredients:

1. 3 eggs
2. 1 cup of sugar
3. 2 tbsp. of butter, melted
4. 1 tbsp. of pure vanilla extract
5. 1 cup of light corn syrup
6. 1 1/2 cups of pecans
7. 1 unbaked 9 inch deep dish pie crust

Preparation:

1. Preheat oven to 350 degrees.
2. Mix eggs, sugar, butter, vanilla, corn syrup, and pecans with a spoon.
3. Pour into a 9-inch piecrust.
4. Bake for 60 - 70 minutes.
5. Allow the pie to cool for 2 hours. The pie is ready when the center is around 200 degrees. If you tap the middle of the piecrust and it bounces back, then the pie is ready. If the piecrust is over-browning before this happens, cover the edges with foil.

Allen Lee Davis

Allen Lee "Tiny" Davis was a prisoner executed in Florida for murdering a pregnant women and her two daughters. The heinous and gruesome photos of the crime are notorious. In fact, the execution, while legal, was criticized afterwards, because Davis bled profusely from the nose while being electrocuted and suffered burns to the head, leg, and groin area. The Florida Supreme Court published photos of the incident that led to heated debate over the use of the electric chair as a form of execution. Currently, because of the controversy surrounding Davis' execution, the electric chair is now an optional form of execution behind lethal injection.

It should be noted that although Davis' nickname was "Tiny," he was in fact morbidly obese and weighed close to 344 pounds at his execution. His attorneys tried, unsuccessfully, to argue that his obesity made it likely that execution by electrocution would constitute cruel and unusual punishment, as protected by the eighth amendment.

Davis was born on July 20, 1944 and was a convict for most of his adult life. An ex-convict convicted of assault and burglary, Davis entered the home of Nancy Weiler, who was at the time pregnant, in Jacksonville, Florida. The gruesome nature of the crime was shocking. Crime scene photos and police officers that responded to the home were unable to visually identify Weiler, as her face was brutally beaten by a gun. Davis also tied Kristina Weiler to a chair and shot her in the face and shot Katherine Weiler in the back as she tried to escape. The amount of blood at the crime scene was staggering, and the gun was left behind at the scene and was damaged because it was used to beat Nancy Weiler.

Davis requested a final meal that consisted of lobster tail, potatoes (fried), fried shrimp, fried claims, garlic bread, and a thirty-two ounce bottle of A&W root beer.

He did not give any final words before his execution by the electric chair. He was the last inmate to be put to death by electrocution in Florida. All subsequent executions in Florida are now implemented using lethal injection.

Allen Lee Davis' Baked Lobster Tail

You don't have to be an expert chef to prepare baked lobster tail at home. What is so special about this recipe is that you require very few ingredients and little time for preparation.

Ingredients:

- 3 lobster tails (of medium size, 8-10 ounces)
- 1 tablespoon of parsley (chopped)
- Pinch of salt
- Olive oil
- 1 teaspoon of lemon juice
- 1 cup of water
- Lemon wedges

Preparation:

- Cut the three lobster tails into equal halves, running through their length. Make sure that you remove the cartilage that covers the tail meat.
- Sprinkle the pieces with the chopped parsley.
- Add salt to the lobster tails before pouring a little olive oil onto them.
- Pour a little lemon juice on each piece separately.
- Place the lobster tails uncovered in a baking pan.
- Bake them at 375 degrees for about 20 to 25 minutes to get them ready for serving. The meat will become firm when they are ready.

- Serve with some lemon wedges.

Stephen Anderson

Stephen Wayne Anderson was born on July 8, 1953 and was a contract killer responsible for carrying out murders for hire and other crimes for criminal organizations and gangs. Anderson was involved in many burglaries and violent crimes during his lifetime, but his murder of 81-year-old Elizabeth Lyman would be the crime that would get him his death sentence.

Anderson had first entered the prison system at the age of eighteen for a count of burglary in 1971 and 3 counts of burglary in 1973. He was convicted in Utah and incarcerated at the Utah State Prison. However, while in state prison, Anderson was convicted of murdering an inmate, assaulting another inmate, and assaulting a correctional officer. Anderson also admitted to killing six other people in Las Vegas before 1981. However, although Anderson was sentenced to life in prison for his crimes, he escaped from prison on November 24, 1979 and subsequently committed another contract killing for narcotics traffickers in Salt Lake County, Utah.

In 1980, Anderson broke into the house of Elizabeth Lyman. During the course of this crime, Anderson cut the telephone line and electricity, but Lyman awoke to find an intruder and screamed. Anderson shot her with a handgun. Attesting to the potential sociopathic nature of the killer, he made himself a meal after killing the woman. A suspicious neighbor called the sheriff's department, and he was arrested while watching television and eating.

The subsequent media firestorm associated with the heinous nature of the crime and the violent history of the defendant led to a death sentence in 1981. However, like most cases in California, the case would go through countless appeals and for the next twenty years would go through the state appeals courts and federal appeals court. Anderson argued his troubled childhood should be a mitigating factor for his crimes and he should have his sentence commuted to life imprisonment.

The state appeals court and federal appeals court would decline his petitions and his original sentence was upheld. Anderson was executed in San Quentin, California for murder and burglary.

Prior to his death, Anderson was granted a last meal request by the prison warden at San Quentin. He received two grilled sandwiches, radishes, a pint of cottage cheese, a slice of peach pie, and a pint of chocolate chip ice cream, and a hominy and corn mixture.

Stephen Anderson's Peach Pie

Ingredients:

- 10 fresh peaches, pitted and sliced
- 1 tbsp. cinnamon
- 1 tbsp. vanilla extract
- 1/3 cup all-purpose flour
- 1 cup of white sugar
- 1/4 cup butter, melted

For the crust:

- 2 1/2 cups all-purpose flour
- 1 cup (2 sticks or 8 ounces) unsalted butter, very-cold, cut into 1/2 inch cubes
- 1 teaspoon salt
- 1 teaspoon sugar
- 6 to 8 tbsp. ice water
- Plastic wrap and rolling pin

Preparation:

1. Preheat the oven to 350. Prepare the piecrust away from the warm area.
2. Combine flour, salt, and sugar in a bowl.
3. Toss ice water until it forms a ball.
4. Knead with your hands until it loosely sticks together.
5. Use a rolling pin to finish the pie dough into flat circles.

6. Toss the peaches in with the remaining ingredients.
7. Put one pie dough circle into a 9-inch pie plate or pan.
8. Spread prepared peaches into the pie plate
9. Top with other crust. Crimp edges together. Poke holes in top with a fork to allow for steam.
10. Bake for 45 minutes or until crust is golden brown. Allow pie to cool and juices to thicken before serving.

Timothy McVeigh

On the surface, Timothy McVeigh would appear to be just like any other citizen. Growing up in Lockport, New York, McVeigh was described as withdrawn and shy. While he had a strong interest and high proficiency in computer programming - hacking into government computer systems while in high school, McVeigh was not remarkably anything.

After dropping out of college, McVeigh, who was intensely interested in gun rights and gun ownership, joined the military after graduating from U.S. Army Infantry School at the age of 20. He served in the first Gulf War and was awarded a Bronze Star for his service, but it is during this war that McVeigh says he began harboring feelings against the United States government.

After returning from the Gulf War, McVeigh attempted to join the United States Army Special Forces but failed to qualify the psychological evaluation, and shortly after, he left the army. After leaving the army, McVeigh became increasingly transient and despondent, working dead-end jobs and racking up gambling debt. All through this however, McVeigh did not give up his anti-government stance. He wrote letters to local newspapers and to the government regarding what he believed was their bloodsucking behavior, and often complained about taxes and the restriction on gun ownership imposed by the government.

During the siege of Waco, McVeigh showed support to the Branch Davidians and their right to bear arms. He distributed pro-gun rights literature at the scene, and it is from there that he started working at gun shows and distributing literature against an FBI sniper involved in the Waco siege.

It was at this point that McVeigh's rhetoric turned radical. He started distributing anti-ATF propaganda, and began experimenting with pipe bombs and other explosive devices on his own. Initially, McVeigh was interested in either attacking a federal official or a federal building, and decided that a federal building would be of the greatest consequence.

After making this decision, McVeigh and co-conspirator Terry Nichols constructed an explosive device and mounted it to the back of a truck. He then drove this truck to the Alfred P. Murrah Federal Building in Oklahoma and lit the fuse for the bomb. After two minutes, an explosion destroyed most of the building and killed 168 people and injured 450 others. Those dead included 19 children who were being hosted in the daycare center in the building.

After the bombing, the FBI traced the Vehicle Identification Number on the truck to a rental agency, which eventually led them to McVeigh. While the FBI was still searching for him, McVeigh was arrested on unrelated charges by Oklahoma police and this led to his indictment on 11 federal counts.

McVeigh's lawyers launched a defense built on McVeigh's actions as a response to the actions of the U.S. government at Waco, Texas. He was found guilty on all 11 counts and the jury recommended the death penalty based on the federal charges brought against McVeigh for the death of eight federal officers who were present in the building at the time. His execution was delayed due to a number of appeals, but McVeigh eventually dropped the appeals, preferring death to spending his life in jail.

On the day of his execution, McVeigh chose his last meal to be two pints of Ben & Jerry's mint chocolate chip ice cream. It is rumored that PETA had contacted McVeigh to request that his final meal contain no meat.

Timothy McVeigh's Ben and Jerry's Mint Chocolate Chip Ice Cream

It's easy to understand why Ben and Jerry's-style mint chocolate chip ice cream has been such a hit, with its wonderful combination of ingredients. When you realize that it's possible to prepare this ice cream at home, it makes the dish even sweeter!

Ingredients:

- 1 can of sweet condensed milk (14oz.)
- 1/2 teaspoon of peppermint extract
- 16 oz. of whipping cream
- 1/2 cup of chocolate chips

Preparation:

- Combine the sweet condensed milk and the whipping cream using a stand mixer on low setting, then increase the speed and continue for around 4 minutes.
- Add the peppermint extract and mix for a further 3 minutes.
- After putting in the chocolate chips, stir the mixture slowly by hand.
- Transfer the mixture to an airtight container.
- Place everything in the freezer for about eight hours to get it ready for serving.

Bruno Richard Hauptmann

Bruno Richard Hauptmann, convicted and executed for the kidnapping and murder of the infant son of aviator Charles Lindbergh, led a tumultuous life of crime that was buffeted by the history of his day.

Born in 1899 in Germany, Hauptmann as a teenager studied carpentry and machine making. The youngest of five children, Hauptmann lost two brothers in World War I before being drafted himself. He served in the German infantry and later claimed both that he had been gassed and that he had suffered a serious head injury that resulted in hours of unconsciousness.

Following the war, Hauptmann commenced a criminal career that began with burglaries. One of the crimes he was convicted of in Germany prefigured his most famous crime: he used a ladder to rob the house of a small town's mayor. Captured and convicted for these thefts, Hauptmann spent three years in jail.

By 1923, Hauptmann was still a young man, but now a former felon. Like many other Europeans at the time (most with honest intentions) he decided to make a fresh start in the U.S. True to form, he immigrated illegally, arriving as a stowaway on a ship that landed in New York.

In New York, Hauptmann seems to have tried to become a law-abiding citizen. He worked as a carpenter, married, and started a family. By 1932, however, he was involved in one of the most notorious crimes of the twentieth century: the Lindbergh kidnapping.

On March 1, 1932, the Lindbergh baby was taken from his bedroom by someone who used a ladder to enter the room and left a ransom note, demanding $50,000. The Lindberghs paid the ransom, but never saw their child alive again. The baby's body was found months later in the woods near the house.

Hauptmann became the main suspect in the search for the murderer and kidnapper when he spent a "gold certificate" at a gas station. Gold certificates were an old-fashioned form of U.S. currency that were being phased out at the time, which was what made the gas station attendant suspicious enough to record Hauptmann's license plate number and call the police.

When police arrived at Hauptmann's home in the Bronx, he led them on a high-speed chase in the city before being captured and arrested. Investigators found over $14,000 of the ransom money in his garage. Hauptmann's trial and conviction relied on forensic evidence. Handwriting experts testified that his handwriting matched the writing on the ransom note. A wood technologist testified that one of the rungs of the hand-made ladder used to enter the house matched a missing piece of wood from the floor of Hauptmann's attic. In addition, numerous witnesses identified him as having spent more of the Lindbergh gold certificates, and the doctor who delivered the ransom identified Hauptmann as the man who had received the money from him.

Hauptmann pleaded innocent and claimed that a German friend (who had since died) had left the money at his house. With the overwhelming evidence against him, however, Hauptmann was convicted and sentenced to death. Hauptmann spent a year on death row in New Jersey, where he received one stay of execution from the governor, who said he believed that others had been involved in the crime. After an alleged co-conspirator was cleared, however, the governor decided not to issue any further stays.

On April 3, 1936, Hauptmann ate his last meal, for which he chose olives and celery, salmon salad, cheese, corn fritters, fruit salad, coffee with milk, and for dessert, cake. He spoke his last words to a minister, reportedly claiming to be completely innocent of the kidnapping and murder. He made no public statement before being put to death in the electric chair of the New Jersey State Prison.

Bruno Richard Hauptmann's Corn Fritters

Corn fritters are great with some bacon and eggs for a filling breakfast.

Ingredients:

- 2 cups of frozen corn
- 1 tablespoon of butter
- 1 egg
- 2/3 of a cup of milk
- 1 tablespoon of oil
- 1 teaspoon of sugar
- 1/2 a teaspoon of salt
- 1 cup of flour
- 2 teaspoons of baking powder

Preparation:

1. Allow the corn to thaw.
2. Mix all remaining ingredients.
3. Add the thawed corn.
4. Heat the oil in a skillet on a medium heat.
5. Drop the mixture in small amounts into the skillet.
6. Turn fritters to allow browning.
7. Drain with a paper towel.
8. Serve.

Clarence Ray Allen

Clarence Ray Allen was executed on January 16, 2006 during his incarceration at San Quentin State Prison in Folsom, California. At 76 years old, he remains one of the oldest death row prisoners to be executed in the United States. He had been found guilty of several murders and sentenced to death in 1980. He was ultimately convicted of the murders of four people.

Allen's choice of a buffalo steak and fry-bread can be linked to his Choctaw heritage and early life in Oklahoma and West Texas. Both are traditional Native American specialties. In his last years, Allen had come to embrace his heritage more strongly. Immediately before his execution, he met with a Native American spiritual advisor. He wore a headband and had an eagle feather with him at the time of his death. However, Allen simply could not resist a bucket of KFC all white meat fried chicken to go with his steak and fry-bread.

He had moved to California as a teenager. He worked as a cotton picker, and married at the age of nineteen. He dabbled in petty crime for most of his life, but eventually built an established and successful security company and raised a family. But in 1974, he was involved in the murder of a young girl, related to an armored robbery that Allen had masterminded. She had exposed Allen's part in the robbery to authorities.

Allen was eventually convicted of the murder and sent to prison with a sentence of life without parole. While he was in prison, Allen plotted the death of several other people involved in his arrest and subsequent conviction. He had a paroled fellow prisoner carry out the executions on his behalf. Billy Ray Hamilton walked into Fran's Market and executed a former witness and two young coworkers with a sawed-off shotgun. He also wounded two others with shotgun blasts. One was another employee who was saved when he put his arm in front of his face, which took most of the impact. He later identified the killer. The second wounded man was a neighbor who returned fire and shot Hamilton, who would be arrested by police one week later after a liquor store robbery. Both Hamilton and Allen were sentenced to death.

For dessert, Allen began with a piece of sugar-free pecan pie. He also asked for walnut ice cream and whole milk. He let the ice cream thaw for an hour, and then made a milkshake by hand. After spending almost thirty years in prison, he certainly would have enjoyed that milkshake. He had diabetes, deafness, blindness, and had recently suffered a heart attack. Although he often used a wheelchair, he walked under his own power to the gurney upon which he would receive a lethal chemical injection. Officials had to administer a second dose of lethal potassium to stop Allen's heart. He was declared dead at 12:38 am.

Clarence Ray Allen's Navaho Fry-Bread

Ingredients:

- 3 cups of flour
- 1/2 a teaspoon of salt
- 1 and 1/2 cups of water (warm)
- 1 tablespoon baking powder
- Some oil

Preparation:

1. Add the baking powder and salt to a bowl, and add the flour.
2. Mix, then add the water.
3. Stir until the dough is like a ball.
4. Flour a surface, and knead the dough.
5. Put it in the fridge for 45 minutes.
6. Heat oil at 350 degrees in a frying pan.
7. Pat down dough mixture and cut a hole in it.
8. Place in oil until browned (3-4 minutes).
9. Flip over and brown the other side
10. Remove excess oil by placing on an excess towel.
11. Serve.

Danny Rolling

Starting in August of 1990, the Southern United States was rocked by the terrifying spree of the Gainesville Ripper, Daniel Harold Rolling.

Rolling started his spree in Gainesville, Florida, 1990. He got his start by breaking into the apartment of two 17-year-old University of Florida Freshmen women. Rolling stabbed, mutilated, and raped the two young women. The most sickening aspect is that one of the victims was raped after being murdered. But Rolling was just getting started - the next day he murdered an 18-year-old woman, and he decapitated and mutilated her body. 48 hours after this third murder, Rolling murdered a 23-year-old woman and her male roommate.

Rolling was finally captured following a failed robbery attempt in the town of Ocala in Florida. This led to a life sentence for armed robbery. Rolling was not initially charged with the Gainesville murders until 1992. He pled guilty to all five charges in 1994. Additionally, DNA evidence linked him to three more murders in Louisiana in 1989, however he was never charged for these crimes.

During his trial, it was posited that Rolling had borderline personality disorder and was at the emotional maturity level of a fifteen-year old. During his incarceration, Rolling became infamous for his "Murderbilia" book, "The Making of a Serial Killer: The True Story of the Gainesville Murders in the Killer's Own Words." Rolling's infamy also gave birth to a book "Beyond Murder." Along with that, his murderous rampage was also the inspiration of the 1996 horror film "Scream." He was also the subject of a 2007 independent film, "The Gainesville Ripper." On top of this, Rolling authored a number of poems, songs, and drawings during his time on death row at Florida State Prison.

On the day of his execution October 26, 2006, the final meal that Daniel Rolling had before making the final walk to his execution consisted of shrimp, lobster tail, a baked potato, strawberry cheesecake, with sweet tea to drink.

Following this final meal, Rolling was sent to the death chamber. Inside the death chamber, Rolling sung hymns while staring at the mother of one of his number of victims. As the lethal cocktail of drugs passed through tubes into his body, he repeated the refrain "None greater than thee oh Lord. None greater than thee." He continued to sing following his microphone being cut off. Not once did he ever appear to be the slightest bit apologetic to the families that he hurt. Thirteen minutes following his singing episode, Daniel Rolling, 52, expired due to the lethal cocktail of drugs injected into his body, making him the 63rd person executed in the state of Florida since 1973.

Danny Rolling's Strawberry Cheesecake

Not many recipes offer the kind of pleasure to prepare like strawberry cheesecake. That's because it's easy to make this mouth-watering stuff at home. Although you require a long list of ingredients for a perfect homemade strawberry cheesecake, the final product compensates for all the hard work that you undertake in preparing these taste-filled cheesecakes.

Ingredients:

- 1 1/2 cups of graham cracker crumbs
- 2 teaspoons of cinnamon
- 1/4 cup of white sugar
- 10 ounces of frozen strawberries
- 1/3 cup of butter
- 1 tablespoon of cornstarch
- 8 ounces of cream cheese
- 14 ounces of condensed milk
- 1/2 teaspoon of vanilla extract
- 1/4 cup of Lemon juice
- 1 tablespoon of water

Preparation:

1. After mixing together the graham cracker crumbs, cinnamon, sugar, and butter, press the mixture onto the bottom of a pan.

2. Refrigerate for about half an hour.
3. Blend strawberries and cornstarch into a puree.
4. Pour this strawberry sauce in a pan; heat it to bring it to a boil.
5. Stir the sauce for a couple of minutes, or until it turns shiny.
6. Allow the sauce to cool, and keep 1/3 of it aside. Refrigerate the rest for serving later.
7. Beat the cream cheese and the condensed milk together till fluffy.
8. Add the vanilla extract and lemon juice, gently beat the product.
9. Beat in the eggs.
10. Pour half of the cream cheese mixture over the crust.
11. Pour the strawberry sauce on the cream cheese layer.
12. Swirl gently with a spoon.
13. Bake in an oven that's preheated to 300 F for about 45 minutes.
14. Allow cake to cool for about an hour.
15. Refrigerate overnight.
16. Serve with the strawberry sauce

Gary Carl Simmons, Jr.

Gary Carl Simmons Jr. was a butcher who took his craft a bit too far in 1996. Simmons was found guilty of carving up Jeffery Wolfe, an already dead man, using his work knives. He then hog-tied the man's girlfriend before viscously raping her. He told her that her life depended on how well she performed sexually for him. This is a sick man in every sense of the word.

Simmons' brother-in-law Timothy Milano initially killed Wolfe over a drug deal gone bad. Once shot dead, Simmons took over, carving him before disposing of his dismembered body in the alligator infested bay.

Simmons Jr. was not at all a model inmate while awaiting his death. He was cited over 60 times while in prison for various infractions, from throwing hot water on the prison staff to sanitary violations. He was actually part of some changes that were made in the system on the treatment and food for those on death row.

Simmons Jr. claimed that while he was awaiting death he made peace with himself and what he had done. On the morning of June 20, 2012, he ordered a light breakfast of eggs and a lunch of meatloaf patty in preparation for what some might say is a caloric record-breaking last meal.

His final meal was a medium-sized deep dish Pizza Hut Super Supreme pizza, 10 packs of parmesan cheese and 10 ranch dressings, a family-sized packet of cheese Doritos, 8 ounces of cheese, 4 ounces of peppers, 2 large milkshakes (strawberry), 2 cherry Cokes, a super-sized McDonald's fries order and 2 pints of ice cream (also strawberry). The caloric intake topped 29,000 and made headlines everywhere.

After the meal and before the lethal injection Simmons Jr. issued this statement, "I've been blessed to be loved by some good people, by some amazing people," Simmons said. "I thank them for their support. Now, let's get it on so these people can go home. That's it." Prison officials said he had a visit from his spiritual advisor and seemed upbeat.

At 6:16 pm that evening at the Mississippi State Penitentiary at Parchman, he was pronounced dead. His victim's father, Mr. Wolfe, was quoted as saying Simmons Jr. was a "piece of trash" who will "burn in hell. When you take your last breath, I'll be going to have a cold beer." While Simmons' family was present, none of them chose to speak at the execution.

Gary Carl Simmons Jr.'s Quick Pizza Hut-style Super Supreme Pizza

If what you're planning is to prepare an inexpensive recipe that guarantees a great taste, then this Pizza Hut-style Quick Super Supreme Pizza recipe is definitely an ideal option. There is little doubt that the homemade pizza will satisfy the stomach. Come holidays, this pizza can be the right choice for the chef and all those who get a slice.

Ingredients:

- 1/2 cup Pepperoni
- 1/2 cup of Ham (cooked)
- 1/2 cup of Italian sausage (cooked)
- 1/2 cup of Pork sausage (cooked)
- 1/2 cup of Button mushrooms
- 1/2 cup of Red onion
- 1/2 cup of Green bell peppers
- 1/2 cup of Black olives
- 1/2 cup of Mozzarella cheese
- Dash of cornmeal
- 1 Pizza base
- Pizza sauce

Preparation:

1. Heat the oven to 450 degrees F.
2. Grease a pizza pan and sprinkle a little cornmeal on it.

3. Pour the pizza sauce over your base, and spread it with a wooden spoon to cover the base.
4. Sprinkle the pepperoni, ham, Italian sausage, pork sausage, mushroom, onion, peppers, and olive over the pizza.
5. Top it with mozzarella cheese.

To ensure that the cheese is melted completely, bake for about 18 minutes. Your favorite Pizza Hut-style Super Supreme Pizza is ready for serving.

John Allen Muhammad

John Allen Muhammad was born on the last day of 1960 and was an American convicted of multiple counts of murder along with his young partner, Lee Boyd Malvo. John Allen Williams was born in Baton Rouge, Louisiana and joined the Nation of Islam in 1987, and changed his name to John Allen Muhammad. Muhammad was responsible for the Beltway sniper attacks that affected Washington DC deeply in 2002. At least 10 people were killed during the attacks, and the case drew widespread media attention and countless law enforcement officials from state police, local police, the FBI, and the ATF were involved in trying to catch Muhammad during that month.

The media speculated that the serial killers were psychopathic; however researchers and criminologists debate this conclusion after the review of Muhammad's psych evaluations.

During the killing spree, Muhammad and Malvo would drive a van around the Beltway and highways and fire a sniper rifle indiscriminately at people doing everyday chores, such as buying groceries, getting gas, or coming out of the office. The apparent randomness of the killings and randomness of the shooting environments created a sense of terror throughout the area before the two were caught.

Muhammad and Malvo were captured in Maryland and tried in U.S. District Court in Virginia at the direct request of the U.S. Attorney General. Some speculate that the change of venue was to ensure a potential death sentence, since Virginia is considered more conservative than Maryland.

Muhammad was charged with murder, terrorism, conspiracy, and the illegal use of a firearm, and represented himself pro se before rehiring counsel after the opening arguments. A year later, Muhammad was convicted of all four counts and sentenced to death. On November 10, 2009, Muhammad was executed by lethal injection after his failed appeals.

Even though Muhammad was convicted and sentenced to death in 2003, the state of Maryland and Virginia tried and convicted Muhammad for state charges related to the crimes committed. Some speculate this was done to ensure any potential successful appeal would be mitigated by existing state convictions.

Unlike some earlier executions, Muhammad's execution and procedures during the execution day are well documented. Documented press reports from interviews with the condemned, lawyers and prison officials stated that Muhammad ate a last meal of chicken with a red sauce and several strawberry cakes before his execution.

John Allen Muhammad's Chicken in Red Sauce

Ingredients:

- 4-6 Chicken Breasts
- 1/4 cup of dry red wine
- 1 1/2 tablespoons of minced garlic
- 1/2 cup of water
- 1/2 cup of maple syrup
- 1/4 cup of brown sugar
- 2 tablespoons of olive oil
- 1 small can of tomato paste
- 1 tablespoon each of: bay leaf, parsley, pepper, thyme and Italian seasoning

Directions:

1. Heat olive oil in a large skillet.
2. Cook garlic until tender.
3. Add chicken breasts to skillet.
4. Cook for about 10 minutes on each side until no longer pink.
5. Mix all ingredients together.
6. Add all ingredients, cover, and simmer for about 20 minutes.
7. Baste chicken with more red wine while cooking.
8. Season to taste with salt and pepper.

Michael Bruce Ross

Michael Bruce Ross was a convicted serial killer and rapist from the Connecticut area. He was accused of the murder and rape of eight girls in New York and Connecticut from the years 1981 to 1984. He was convicted by jury for four of those eight alleged murders.

According to testimony by his sister, Ross was abused by his angry mother. His mother would abuse all of the children physically, but he likely received most of the abuse. His mother once abandoned the family, and was institutionalized. Ross was likely molested by an uncle who later committed suicide. After his uncle's suicide, Michael would strangle chickens by hand while working on the farm.

Ross was quite intelligent, and was educated at Cornell University in Ithaca where he pursued studies in agriculture. He was later employed as an insurance salesperson. However, there were hints of his violent and antisocial behavior in college. It was here that he began to rape. In 1982 he assaulted a pregnant police officer's wife, but was only fined and given probation.

Ross graduated to strangling and murdering women soon after the assault. His first would be Robin Stavinsky in 1983. Stavinsky was memorialized as a star track athlete with so much potential. She was followed by the double murder of April Brunais and Leslie Shelley on Easter Sunday of 1984. These two girls were only 14 at the time of their murders. Ross killed Wendy Baribeault two months later.

Ross was convicted and executed for four murders although he confessed to a total of eight. He was noted for making positive strides after his imprisonment in 1984 including aiding other inmates and sponsoring a child while incarcerated. It was his full-on conversion to Catholicism that seemed to shape a lot of the positive attributes post-arrest. His Catholic alliances gave cause for the Norwich Diocese to publicly seek signatures for petitions to lobby the Connecticut legislature to end public executions. Connecticut as a state is somewhat reluctant towards execution, having not executed anyone prior to Ross since 1960.

Even with Ross's open acceptance of his own execution for the purposes of alleviating victim's suffering, his execution wouldn't come until 2005. This delay was somewhat lengthened by Ross's father and attorneys fighting diligently for appeal. This meant that the stay on death row was nearly 20 years, and this contributed to the common opinion that Ross had death row syndrome - he wanted to die.

Ross was somewhat unique in that he didn't request a special last meal. He ended up eating the prison "meal of the day" - turkey a la king, mixed vegetables, rice, bread, and fruit.

Michael Bruce Ross' Turkey a la King

Ingredients:

- 1/4 cup and 2 tbs. of butter
- 2 minced shallots
- 1/8 cup flour
- 1/3 cup cooking sherry
- 4 cups chicken broth
- 3 tbs. parsley
- 3 teaspoons thyme
- 1 teaspoon salt
- 1/2 teaspoon black pepper
- Pinch of cayenne pepper
- Pinch of nutmeg
- 1/2 pound shiitake mushrooms, chopped
- 1/2 cup heavy cream or crème fraiche
- 2 chicken breasts
- 1 tablespoon chives

Directions:

1. Put a large pan on the stove and heat it to medium heat.
2. Sauté the shallots in a 1/4 of a cup of melted butter until they are soft. This should take about 5 minutes.
3. Sprinkle in some flour and stir it in.
4. Add sherry and broth, stirring until it comes to a boil.
5. Add thyme and parsley and lower the heat to simmer.

6. Let cook for 30 minutes, not forgetting to stir.
7. Use the leftover butter to sauté the mushrooms for about 5 minutes, adding some salt and pepper.
8. Add salt, pepper, nutmeg and cayenne to the mushrooms after straining in the sauce.
9. Use a whisk to add the crème fraiche.
10. Preparing the chicken: add chicken breast, the carrot, celery, parsley, thyme, and onion to a pan covered with broth that is about boiling.
11. Change the heat to low and cover the pan.
12. Cook for 20 minutes.
13. Take the pan off the stove and let it sit for 1/2 an hour.
14. Cut the chicken into cubes.
15. Add the parsley, chicken, and chives to the sauce, and simmer.
16. Serve.

Rainey Bethea

Rainey Bethea was a black man born in Roanoke, Virginia around 1909. Rainey was an orphan since the age of ten, and worked as a laborer for many years, even living in one family's basement for a year. Although eventually being convicted of the rape and murder of a seventy-year-old white woman, his life was markedly free of crime up until 1935. In 1935, he was charged with a breach of peace, as well as being convicted of theft.

Bethea is most notable for being the last criminal in the United States to be publicly executed. He was killed by hanging in 1936 in Owensboro, Kentucky. As a result of the media firestorm brought about by mistakes in his hanging, his death was, in some regards, responsible for the end of public executions.

Bethea's crime occurred in 1936 on June 7. Bethea gained access to seventy-year-old Lischia Edwards' bedroom through a window, with the intent to rob her. Before taking some of her personal belongings, he choked and raped Lischia Edwards, leaving her in the bedroom. While he escaped unnoticed, he did make one mistake in committing the crime, as he left his prison ring in her bedroom. The ring, when later discovered alongside the body by Ms. Edwards' downstairs neighbors, played a pivotal role in the conviction of Bethea.

Bethea's arrest was handled very gingerly by the police, who were afraid of a lynch mob starting if word got out that the murderer had been captured. Bethea confessed multiple times to the crime while on trial, deciding to plead guilty before the trial had even begun. The defense did not even counter-examine or cross-examine any of the twenty-one witnesses who were brought forward to testify against him.

Bethea's hanging became national news because of the fact that the sheriff was a female. Bethea was executed on August 14 at sunrise. It's estimated that a crowd of nearly twenty thousand onlookers gathered to see the hanging in an abandoned lot. As it was the first execution of a man by a female sheriff, many newspaper reporters took great liberties when reporting the execution.

Bethea was buried in a pauper's grave in Owensboro, against his wishes to be sent to South Carolina, where his sister lived. While Bethea had little to say on the day of his execution, and issued no public statement before his hanging, it can be inferred from the last meal that Rainey ordered that he was seeking both solace and comfort. Many components of Bethea's last meal contain popular southern comfort foods, such as the pork chops and fried chicken. Additionally, Bethea's final meal included cornbread, mashed potatoes, and even pickled cucumbers, other southern favorites. For dessert, Bethea was served both lemon pie and ice cream. The entire meal was served to him at four o'clock in the afternoon the day before his execution.

Rainey Bethea's Lemon Pie

There are certain recipes that you feel like trying at home the very first time you taste them. Lemon pie is definitely one such prominent recipe. Blessed with terrific taste and unique flavor, lemon pie is an ideal recipe to prepare and serve to family members and friends

Ingredients:

- 1/2 cup of lemon juice
- 1/4 cup of sugar
- 9-inch pie crust (baked)
- 4 eggs
- 14 ounces of sweetened condensed milk
- 1 lemon's zest

Preparation:

1. Separate the yellow and white portion of the eggs.
2. Preheat the oven to 350 F.
3. Mix lemon juice, condensed milk, lemon zest, and 2 egg yolks in a mixing bowl.
4. Pour the mixture into the pie shell.
5. Combine the sugar and the 4 egg whites in a bowl, and best till peaks begin to form.
6. Add this meringue over the mixture in the pie shell.
7. Bake it for about 10 minutes, or such time as it turns golden brown.

That's it, your lemon pie is ready! (Note, you'll have 2 egg yolks left over). You can also vanilla flavoring to give it a distinctive taste.

Velma Barfield

In the case of Velma Barfield, the last meal may be considered a tongue in cheek nod to the irony of last meals. She chose only a bag of cheese doodles and a can of Coca-Cola. Why did she choose those two things out of all the many things she could have chosen?

Barfield was called the "death row granny," since she was in her 60's when she was executed, and also a grandmother. She was convicted for the poisoning murder of her boyfriend Stuart Taylor. She put arsenic in his beer and tea because she said she was afraid he would find out she had written bad checks on his accounts.

Barfield, unfortunately, had been a drug addict since her hysterectomy several years before. A wave of deaths followed her wherever she went after that, starting with her first husband. Her second husband also died under mysterious circumstances. Then, both of her parents died after she moved in with them. That was not all though. Barfield made her living caring for elderly couples, and not one, but two sets of elderly couples died of "stomach viruses" or other causes under her care.

Taylor was the last death, and the most suspicious. His daughter would not rest until the mysteriousness surrounding her father's early demise was solved.

Barfield, despite being championed by Billy Graham, never had her death sentence commuted to life in prison. She claimed to be a born again Christian and to have found God. She also claimed childhood abuse, spousal abuse, and multiple personalities. The judge in her case would not be swayed for any of these reasons. She was the only woman on death row in the North Carolina Central Prison where she was staying prior to her execution. She was the first woman to be executed since the 1976 re-instatement of the death penalty and the first woman to ever be executed by lethal injection.

After murdering more than a half dozen people in her life, Barfield was finally caught and convicted. Her murder spree covered up her check frauds to pay for her drug habit and her ineptness in caring for the elderly people in her charge.

She was executed on December 2 1978. Perhaps because of an ironic fear of being poisoned herself, she chose as her last meal two things that came in packages, packaged foods being harder to fill with poison than prepared foods. Cheese doodles and Coca-Cola may have just been her favorite foods or foods that were often denied her in prison.

Barfield ate her cheese doodles and drank her Coca-Cola, and got to see whether God really did forgive her for her crimes.

Velma Barfield's Spicy Cheese Doodle-style Snacks

Ingredients:

- 1 pkg. frozen puff-pastry, thawed
- 1 egg, beaten
- 8 oz. of pepper jack cheese, shredded
- 1/4 cup of grated parmesan cheese and a little more for sprinkling
- 1 tablespoon of smoked paprika
- 2 teaspoons garlic powder
- 1/2 teaspoon of cayenne pepper
- 1 teaspoon of kosher salt

Directions:

1. Preheat oven to 375.
2. In a small bowl, combine the smoked paprika, garlic powder, cayenne pepper, parmesan, and kosher salt.
3. Roll one pastry sheet into a large square.
4. Brush the pastry sheet with beaten egg.
5. Sprinkle half the spice mixture and half the pepper jack cheese on the square of pastry.
6. Fold the pastry in half and lightly roll over the pastry, sealing the cheese and spices inside.
7. Cut the pastry into thin strips.
8. Twist each strip and place on a parchment paper-lined cookie sheet.

9. Press the ends against the parchment paper to keep the strips from untwisting.
10. Sprinkle with more parmesan cheese.
11. Bake until golden and puffy, about 20 minutes.
12. Remove and let cool.
13. Repeat with the second puff pastry sheet and remaining ingredients.
14. Store in an airtight container or large Ziploc bag.

William Bonin

William George Bonin was born January 8, 1947. He was one of three children, with parents who both were alcoholics. Bonin's grandfather, a convicted child molester, was often left to tend to the three boys.

It was at the age of 10 that Bonin would begin his life of crime, and only a few short years later when he would start molesting children. Bonin would go on to graduate high school and join the U.S. Air Force. While a dedicated soldier, Bonin would later admit to sexually assaulting two other soldiers while in the Vietnam War.

He left the force in 1968 and moved to California. This would be the same year when Bonin would be convicted of sexually assaulting a child at the age of 21. During the next year Bonin would kidnap and sexually assault four more children. He was convicted of each of these attacks and sent to a mental hospital. Later he would be sent to prison, however, with the hospital stating they were unable to treat him.

Released from prison in 1974, it would take just 16 short months for Bonin to once again commit the very same act that put him away in the first place. This time Bonin raped, at gunpoint, a 14-year old runaway boy. This sent him back to serve an 18-month prison sentence. Upon his release he met a couple of co-workers who would eventually help in the assaults and attacks on these young boys. Upon this release Bonin would begin picking up hitchhikers, sexually assaulting and killing them. He was nicknamed 'The Freeway Killer' for this reason.

He was captured in 1980 and confessed to killing a total of 21 young men. Two other men, whom Bonin had met after his second release from prison, were also arrested and charged with the murders of several hitchhikers who had been killed in the area. During trial Bonin would be convicted of 14 of the 21 confessed killings, for which he was sentenced to death.

He would sit on death row for more than 17 years before execution would take place, thanks to appeals. It was noted that while in prison Bonin told a reporter that he enjoyed killing, and had he not been caught would certainly still be out there doing it.

Bonin was killed by lethal injection on February 23, 1996. He was the first person in California to be killed by lethal injection. Bonin's last meal consisted of 15 Coca Colas, 2 pepperoni and sausage pizzas, and 3 servings of chocolate ice cream. His execution took longer than usual, due to a problem finding a vein for the injection. Bonin was pronounced dead at 12:13 a.m. February 23, 1996, 12 minutes after the process was scheduled to start.

William Bonin's Pepperoni and Sausage Pizza

Eating becomes fun when you have something like pepperoni and sausage pizza on the table! Preparing this unique pizza at home is a simple task.

Ingredients:

- 1 pizza crust
- 1/2 a cup of pizza sauce
- 1/4 teaspoon of basil
- 1/4 teaspoon of thyme
- 1/4 teaspoon of salt
- 1/4 teaspoon of oregano
- 1/4 teaspoon of black pepper
- 1/2 a pepperoni (sliced)
- 1 Italian sausage
- 6 ounces of mozzarella cheese

Preparation:

1. Preheat the oven to 350 degrees F.
2. Heat a skillet to a medium heat.
3. In the skillet, cook the Italian sausage until brown.
4. Set the sausage aside till later.
5. Spread the sauce over the pizza base, and sprinkle with the herbs.
6. Arrange the mozzarella slices across the pizza.
7. Drizzle the sausage and pepperoni over the cheese.

8. Bake for around 9 minutes or until the cheese is fully melted.
9. Allow pizza to cool for a few minutes.

Your favorite pepperoni and sausage pizza is now ready to serve.

Eric Wrinkles

Matthew "Eric" Wrinkles was born on January 3, 1960 and was convicted of murdering his wife, his brother in law, and his sister in law in 1994.

Matthew Wrinkles was married to Debbie Wrinkles. After a constantly rocky marriage, Debbie decided to move in with her brother Tony and his wife Natalie in Evansville. Soon after, Debbie Wrinkles filed for divorce and sought a protective order from her ex-husband. In July, they met across a lawyer's table and decided to put the protective order to the side, allowing Matthew Wrinkles rights of visitation.

Later that same night, however, Wrinkles would commit the triple homicide that would put him on death row. He parked his car around the block, cut the home's telephone connection, and barged in the back door. Armed with a handgun and wielding a knife, he shot Natalie in the face and Tony four times in the chest, face, hip, and back. He then proceeded to shoot his ex-wife Debbie in her chest and shoulder area. One of the children, who saw the shooting, attempted CPR on her mother.

Later, Wrinkles was found and arrested in his cousin's home with the murder weapon. During the trial, Wrinkles sought to claim a defense of mental disease and defect, as he was committed prior to the incident by his mother for a psychological evaluation. Even though he was discharged from the hospital, Wrinkles claimed he was not responsible for his actions because of his mental illness. This defense was rejected, and in following appeals it was not grounds for a retrial.

Wrinkles was convicted of triple homicide and sentenced to death. On November 3, 2009, his appeals were denied and clemency applications were rejected by the governor of Indiana. Wrinkles as executed in November 2009. The most notable part of Wrinkles' execution was his apparent complacence and acceptance of the execution. In fact, Wrinkles did not resist.

Wrinkles was executed in Indiana for his crimes. Unlike most states, Indiana grants its condemned a last meal request three days prior to an execution. The rationale, according to Indiana State Penitentiary officials, is that prisoners lose his or her appetite the day of the execution. As such, it was decided to grant condemned inmates a last meal in advance. Wrinkles ate a meal of prime rib, a baked potato, pork chops, steak fries, two salads, and accompanying dressing.

Eric Wrinkles' Baked Potato

The key ingredient in homemade baked potatoes is the potato. You will want a good-sized, fresh potato.

Ingredients:

- 1 large baked potato
- Butter
- Toppings to taste

Preparation:

- Wash the potato.
- Preheat the oven to 400 degrees.
- Poke a few holes in it using a fork.
- Wrap the potato in foil.
- Bake the potato in the oven for between 30-45 minutes. (You can also cut the potato in half to afford a faster cooking time.)
- After the potato is cooked and removed from the oven, it is ready for its toppings. There are countless toppings to put on a potato. Typical toppings include: butter, cheese, chives, bacon bits, and sour cream. You can also add meats such as barbecue brisket, or grilled chicken for a more exotic baked potato.

Printed in Great Britain
by Amazon.co.uk, Ltd.,
Marston Gate.